21st
Century
Skills Library

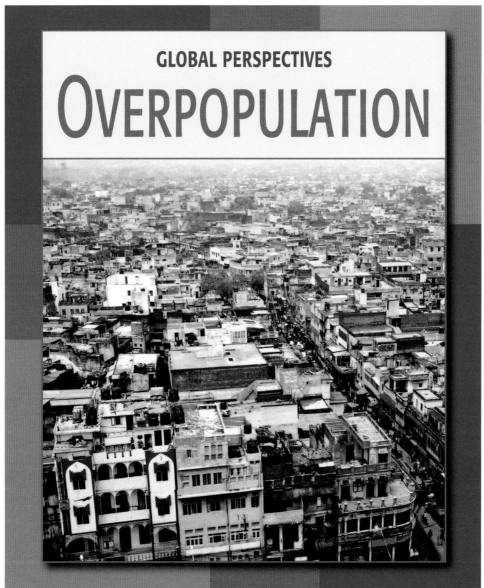

GLOBAL PERSPECTIVES

OVERPOPULATION

Robert Green

Cherry Lake Publishing
Ann Arbor, Michigan

CHERRY LAKE
Publishing

Published in the United States of America by Cherry Lake Publishing
Ann Arbor, Michigan
www.cherrylakepublishing.com

Content Adviser: Pam Wasserman, Director of Education, Population Connection, Washington, DC.

Photo Credits: Cover and page 1, © iStockphoto.com/miteman; page 4, © Li Wa, used under license from Shutterstock, Inc.; page 7, © iStockphoto.com/picha; page 8, © James B. Adson, used under license from Shutterstock, Inc.; page 9, © Images&Stories/Alamy; page 12, © Gary Cook/Alamy; page 13, © David Levenson/Alamy; page 15, © Karl Naundorf, used under license from Shutterstock, Inc.; page 16, © Bill Brooks/Alamy; page 18 and 26, © Charlotte Thege/Alamy; page 21, © Brian Atkinson/Alamy; page 22, © Keren Su/China Span/Alamy; page 24, © Patker Photo Agency/Alamy

Map by XNR Productions Inc.

Library of Congress Cataloging-in-Publication Data
Green, Robert, 1969–
  Overpopulation / by Robert Green.
    p. cm.— (Global perspectives)
  ISBN-13: 978-1-60279-127-5
  ISBN-10: 1-60279-127-9
  1. Overpopulation—Juvenile literature. I. Title. II. Series.
  HB883.G74 2008
  363.9'1—dc22   2007035729

*Cherry Lake Publishing would like to acknowledge the work of
The Partnership for 21st Century Skills.
Please visit www.21stcenturyskills.org for more information.*

TABLE of CONTENTS

CHAPTER ONE

Rubbing Elbows in Hong Kong   4

CHAPTER TWO

When It Becomes Too Crowded   9

CHAPTER THREE

Are People the Problem?   13

CHAPTER FOUR

Managing a Growing Population   18

CHAPTER FIVE

Some Difficult Questions   22

Map   28

Glossary   30

For More Information   31

Index   32

About the Author   32

CHAPTER ONE

RUBBING ELBOWS IN HONG KONG

Hong Kong has a population of about 6.9 million people.
Most people live in high-rise apartment buildings.

Emma Kwan stood at the window of the Hong Kong Convention Center, looking at the activity swirling in front of her.

"I just can't believe all the people," said Asger Knudsen, a student from the northern European country of Denmark who stood next to her. "It looks like there are more people in the city of Hong Kong than in all of Denmark."

"In fact," said Emma, "there are. More people live in the small territory of Hong Kong than in all of the land of Denmark. Here you will see people everywhere rubbing elbows as they travel through the streets and on subways and buses."

Asger was amazed. "How do you know so much about how many people there are in different countries?" he asked.

"Well, it might be an unusual hobby, but I like **demography**," she said. "It is the scientific study of populations and the factors that affect them."

When a census taker visits houses in your neighborhood, you are seeing demographers in action. The census is a periodic count of the number of people in the country. But census takers do not count everyone. They do a sampling by looking at certain areas and the movement of people. Then they do the math. By using formulas, demographers can estimate the size of a population and estimate how big it will be in the future. This information affects many things, from taxes to government policy. Demographers help us understand what we look like as a group. Do you think you would enjoy working as a demographer? If you do, you will need to be very interested in people. You will also need to study math and science.

"And how do you know so much about Hong Kong?" asked Asger.

"I grew up here," said Emma proudly. "And it is a fantastic place to study people!"

Emma's hobby might have been demographics, but her job for this day was to welcome students, such as Asger, to her home city. They arrived in teeming Hong Kong for the International Global Issues workshop, and they were assigned to a group studying the problem of overpopulation.

"Would you say that Hong Kong is overpopulated?" asked Asger.

"That is one of the questions we have to figure out," said Emma. "There is a very lively debate over the effects of population growth and the crowding in cities."

✳ ✳ ✳

In general, overpopulation refers to the growth of the human population to a size at which it causes problems for people or their environment. When there are so many people in one area that it becomes difficult for them to find enough food, shelter, or fresh water, that area is overpopulated. An area can also be overpopulated if residents of a specific place, like Hong Kong, begin to suffer a decline in the quality of their lives. This can happen if the city becomes too noisy or the air becomes polluted. It can also happen if there is not enough housing to squeeze all the people into the city.

Water is an important natural resource.

On a larger scale, demographers also ask if the **natural resources** on Earth can support all of the people on the planet. Those natural resources include fresh water, fresh air, and food. They also include energy resources, such as oil, natural gas, and coal.

✳ ✳ ✳

Tokyo has a population of more than 12 million people.
It is the most densely populated city in Japan.

"Does that mean that the number of people on Earth or in an area is not the only factor that determines overpopulation?" asked Asger.

"That's right!" said Emma, truly happy that she finally had a chance to share her interest in demographics. "Over the next week, we will look at the history of population growth and the problems of overpopulation. Then we will look at some of the ideas for solving the problem of overpopulation."

CHAPTER TWO

WHEN IT BECOMES TOO CROWDED

Bangladesh is one of the most densely populated countries in the world.
Some people there have trouble finding enough food and clean water.

"If it isn't just a question of the number of people, how do we measure overpopulation?" asked Asger.

"To answer that, we need to look at the number of people compared to the space in which they live," said Emma. "This is known as **population density**, or the number of people in a given area."

At this point, Emma and Asger stopped chatting as a boy from the South Asian nation of Bangladesh rose to give a presentation. Bangladesh has one of the highest population densities in the world. Its overall population is about 150 million people. For a comparison, the United States, the world's third most populated nation, has about 300 million people or about double the population of Bangladesh. But the people of Bangladesh are squeezed into an area slightly smaller than the single U.S. state of Iowa. Bangladesh, in other words, has a high population density—it has a lot of people living in a small area.

"The effects of overpopulation on Bangladesh are enormous," began Jafar Razzak, the Bangladeshi speaker. "We sometimes have a shortage of food. We have trouble finding enough clean water. And so many people are without homes that they live on the dangerous flood plains near the Sea of Bengal. These plains flood often. Houses are destroyed, and people are washed out to sea."

❋ ❋ ❋

Because Bangladesh has such a high population density, it is often used by demographers to study overpopulation. Bangladesh exhibits many of the symptoms of overpopulation. Although the country has plenty of land for farming, it does not always produce enough food for its people. The environment also suffers from the large population. **Pesticides** used in farming pollute water sources. The cutting down of trees worsens flooding. Disease spreads during the floods, and many people lack basic social services, such as access to hospitals and medicines.

Population growth is not evenly distributed over the globe. The population of Bangladesh continues to grow at a rate of about 2 percent per year. This is a high population growth rate. Other countries, such as Japan and some Western European countries, have negative growth rates. Their populations are actually shrinking.

Worldwide, however, population continues to rise. From 1959 to 1999, the world's population

If you look at a map that shows human population around the world, you will see that people cluster in certain areas. These areas tend to be near seacoasts or situated on rivers. The water was once the "highway" on which goods and people traveled. So cities developed on or near seacoasts and rivers to take advantage of being near transportation. But why do people gather in cities and put up with all that crowding? One answer is jobs. There tends to be more economic activity in cities, and people move there to get jobs. Can you think of any other reasons why people would move to cities?

One reason people settle near rivers is that transporting goods by boat is often quicker than moving them over land.

doubled, rising from 3 billion to 6 billion. In 2007, there were already another 600 million people in the world.

✳ ✳ ✳

"As the population of Bangladesh grows," Jafar concluded, "living conditions will decline further. And as the world's population continues to grow, other countries will also struggle with the problems of overpopulation."

CHAPTER THREE

ARE PEOPLE THE PROBLEM?

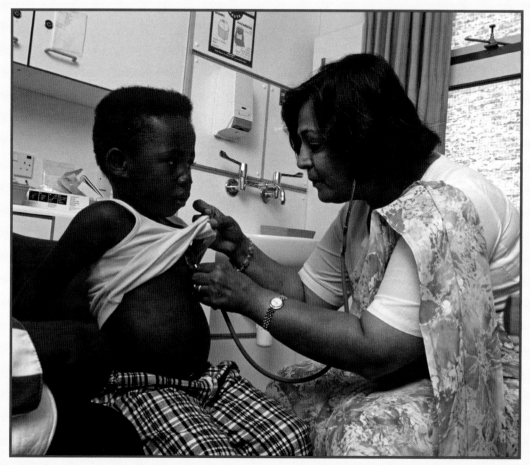

Access to good health care is sometimes difficult in overcrowded countries.

After Jafar finished his speech, a young man from England named James Brudenell stood up to give the other side of the argument. He disagreed with many of the things that Jafar had said.

"People," said James, "are not the problem. Problems like access to clean water or health care are not caused by overpopulation. They are the result of poor government planning and an underdeveloped economy. Hong Kong has a higher population density than Bangladesh, but it does not have the same problems as Bangladesh. In England, we had a remarkable thinker named Thomas Malthus. In 1798, he predicted that population growth would lead to starvation all over the world. He was as intelligent as Jafar, but he was equally wrong."

James presented a different point of view than Jafar. He was turning the conference into a debate. In a debate, people argue their point of view and give evidence to support it. James was right about Thomas Malthus. This famous thinker and early demographer predicted that space for farming would decline as the population grew. He believed that eventually there would be too many people to feed.

※ ※ ※

Thomas Malthus was a very intelligent man, but he had missed one possibility that turned out to make all the difference. As the population grew, people learned how to grow food more efficiently. They crossbred different crops to make them more resistant to disease. They used new farming techniques. They also developed new pesticides to kill the bugs and diseases that damage crops. Food production grew faster than the population.

Even if a highly populated country has a lot of good farmland, its farmers may not be able to grow enough food to feed all of the country's people.

Today, many countries in the world produce more food than their populations need. But in Bangladesh, even though there is much land that is good for farming, it isn't enough. There is only 0.15 acre (0.06 hectare) of good farmland per person.

Smog fills the air over a highway in Canada.
Cars are one source of air pollution.

There is an important lesson to be learned from the predictions of Thomas Malthus. Humans can change their environment in all sorts of ways through **innovation** and **technology**. The new farming techniques that dramatically increased the food supply are proof of this.

Some people argue that even the environmental problems, such as air and water **pollution**, can be solved. They say that pollution happens because of the way people do things, not because there are too many people to keep the world clean. So, for example, it is true that more people driving cars will lead to more exhaust puffing out of car tailpipes. But some people argue that the invention of cleaner-burning fuels can reduce pollution, even if there are more people on Earth.

* * *

"So you see," said James, "the problem is not how many people we have, but how they are doing things. The population can continue to grow, and we can solve problems like those in Bangladesh through innovation and through good government policy."

"But surely," said Asger, "the population can't continue to grow forever!" And this was a point that all of the students started thinking about. After all, space on Earth is limited.

Demographers calculate the demographic age of a country. This is the average of the ages of all the people in the country. Japan and some European countries, for example, are elderly, meaning that there are more elderly people than young people. In other countries, like many in the Middle East, there are more young people than elderly people. These statistics, or numerical facts, help predict the future growth of the population in certain areas. They also have very important consequences for the people who live in those places.

Why do you think the demographic age of a country is important for people studying population? What kinds of problems would a young country have that an elderly country would not? What problems would an elderly country face that a young country would not?

CHAPTER FOUR

MANAGING A GROWING POPULATION

Two children harvest tea leaves on their family's farm in Kenya. Families tend to have more children in countries with economies based on farming.

"**I**, for one, don't think that Hong Kong could take many more people," said Emma. "And the population keeps growing. I'm not sure how that can be managed."

"Leaders must be careful to consider all of the things that make population grow," said James. "Remember that population growth is not driven just by the number of children born, but also by people moving from place to place. Why do people come to Hong Kong? It is often in search of jobs and a better life."

James had hit on one issue that makes population change a truly global question. That issue is **migration**, the movement of people from one place to another. As he said, people often move to find work.

*** * ***

There is a connection between **economic development** and population growth. Countries that are less economically developed, such as Bangladesh or Indonesia, tend to have greater population growth. Countries that are more highly developed economically, such as Japan, the United States, and Western European nations, tend to have lower population growth.

One approach to easing the problems of overpopulation relies on helping a country develop its economy. The number of children per family tends to decrease as a country's economy changes from one based on farming to one that is based on industry, manufacturing, and trade. This is often because it is useful to have many children when they are needed to work on the family farm. But if you live in a city, it can be too expensive to find housing for a large family.

When people cross into another country, they are known as immigrants. Their journey can be beneficial for both the migrant and the host country. In the United States, for example, many Mexicans cross into the United States to work. They help harvest crops and fill a gap in the workforce. The U.S. economy depends on immigrants. They help keep the economy moving and provide labor to U.S. businesses.

Immigration is still controversial, however. Some migrants come legally, while others come illegally. Immigrants also bring their own languages and traditions. Some people find that this enriches U.S. society. But other people argue that immigrants take jobs from people who already live in the United States. They also argue that immigrants change the nature of U.S. culture, and this makes them uncomfortable. The bottom line is that many U.S. businesses could not survive without the inexpensive labor provided by immigrants from Mexico and elsewhere.

Population distribution has also tended to change over time as the world's borders have become more flexible. As European countries began to decline in population growth, they discovered that they needed more workers to fill jobs. These workers are often immigrants, or economic migrants in search of jobs. In the larger picture, people tend to move from more populated, economically underdeveloped areas to less-populated but highly developed economies.

✳ ✳ ✳

"I get it!" said Asger. "Overpopulation solves itself when people move from one place to another."

James raised an eyebrow at this conclusion. "It's not quite that simple," he said. "Everybody can't just pick up and move, and countries can't just take every new person who wants to come. This is

A migrant worker from Guatemala works with a Canadian worker on a farm in Canada. Many people leave their home countries in search of work.

the political part of the problem. Countries have policies on immigration, and they do not always allow people to move from one place to another. As a result, there are many government programs all over the world that attempt to control population growth."

CHAPTER FIVE

SOME DIFFICULT QUESTIONS

Crowds of people fill the streets of a shopping district in Shanghai, China.

Asger finally understood the debate over the dangers of overpopulation. He also realized that there is agreement among most world leaders that **population policies** should be created to manage the problem of overpopulation. "But how," asked Asger, "do governments manage population growth?"

"Oh," said Emma, jumping at the chance to relate one of her favorite demographic topics, "I can tell you about the most famous population policy program in history. China is the most populated country in the world. In the late 1950s, Chinese leaders created a plan to modernize the country and quickly advance its economy. They wanted to create jobs and wealth for the Chinese people. This was known as the Great Leap Forward. It was a giant failure and ended in starvation and suffering for many people. As a result, the Chinese government attempted to attack the problem from another direction—by limiting population growth."

✵ ✵ ✵

The inability of the Chinese government to provide enough jobs and services for its people led to the creation of a strong population policy, known as the "one-child policy." During the 1970s, the government urged people to have fewer children. By 1979, the policy included punishments for people who had more than one child.

China's attempt at controlling the country's population growth was very successful. People began to have fewer children, and today China's population growth is slowing. In a few decades, China's population will begin to shrink. There will be more elderly people dying off than there are new children being born.

Some people, however, say that the government should not have a right to tell people how many children to have. These objections make population policies controversial. These people say that the one-child policy violates **human rights**. They argue that people have the right to decide how many children

A wedding is celebrated in the city of Persepolis, Iran. In an effort to slow population growth, the Iranian government requires couples to take a pre-marriage class in family planning.

they want to have, and no government should take away that right.

China's population policy is an extreme form of **family planning**. Other countries encourage family planning with less extreme methods. In 1950, families in Mexico had an average of seven children. Today, the average Mexican family has two to three children. This decrease was accomplished by encouraging people to plan their families. It became acceptable to use natural and medical means to prevent pregnancy.

In Iran, the average number of children per family in the late 1980s was seven. Then leaders raised the minimum age for marriage. Those getting married received family planning education. Medical services that help prevent pregnancy were also made more available. Today, families there have an average of two children.

Family planning is voluntary almost everywhere. Couples can decide whether or not they want to try to prevent pregnancy. Family planning policies, however, can still cause arguments. Government leaders may firmly believe that promoting family planning is necessary to keep their country's population at a manageable level. Some people, however, believe that nothing should interfere with the creation of new life. When people on both sides of a question hold strong views, it can make it difficult for a government to establish a population policy.

It isn't just family planning policies, however, that help lower birth rates. Population growth rates are highest in countries where girls have little education, few opportunities to work outside the home, and cannot vote or hold political office. Birth

How many people is too many? Scientists who study ecosystems—communities of living things and their environments—know that every ecosystem has a carrying capacity. The carrying capacity of an ecosystem is the maximum number of a specific living thing that it can support. If an ecosystem goes over its carrying capacity, there won't be enough food, water, and other resources to go around.

Think of your family's home as an ecosystem. How many people do you think that ecosystem can support? What is the maximum number of people you think could live in your home? Would you want that many people living in your home? Why or why not?

A young girl helps her mother grind grain in Tanzania. In many developing countries, girls drop out of school to help with housework.

rates remain high in countries where daughters are not valued as highly as sons. In these countries, many girls drop out of school to help work in the home. They also marry young and begin having children at a young age. But when girls stay in school and have opportunities to work outside the home, family size tends to decrease.

The solutions to the problems caused by overpopulation are not simple. There are no easy answers. Governments and people need to work together to determine what they think has the best chance of making a difference.

In the meantime, we can reduce the harm caused by people to our environment. We can do this by relying on innovation. For example, using sunlight to create energy could help reduce pollution and provide energy for a growing population. Farming methods that keep the soil healthy will allow farmers to grow more food to feed more people. These are examples of **sustainable development**, things that we can do to make sure that Earth's growing population doesn't harm the environment.

✹ ✹ ✹

"So you mean that as the debate on overpopulation continues, we still need to find new ways to live together and prevent the problems of having too many people?" asked Asger.

"That's exactly right," said Jafar, thinking of his native Bangladesh with its many people and the problems they face. "One thing is for certain, we need to find ways to make people's lives better. I still think we should limit population growth!"

"And I think that we had better find ways to solve humanitarian problems like hunger and environmental problems like pollution," said James. "We need more economic development and more education. That is the answer."

Emma, sensing an argument brewing, gave the last word on the subject. "Perhaps," she said, "we could do both."

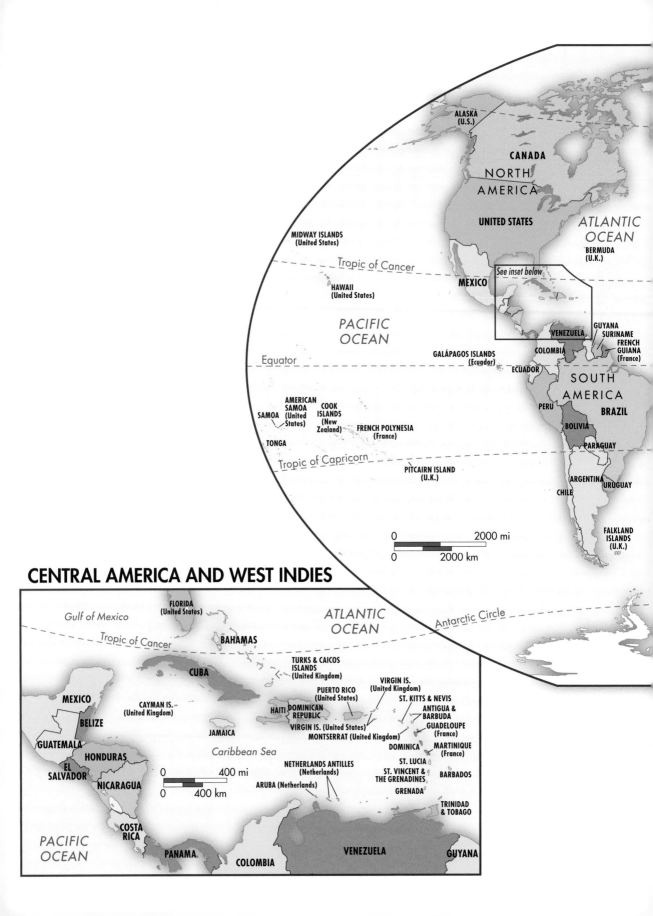

ALASKA
(U.S.)

CANADA

NORTH
AMERICA

UNITED STATES

ATLANTIC
OCEAN

BERMUDA
(U.K.)

MIDWAY ISLANDS
(United States)

Tropic of Cancer

HAWAII
(United States)

See inset below

MEXICO

PACIFIC
OCEAN

GUYANA
SURINAME
FRENCH
GUIANA
(France)

VENEZUELA

COLOMBIA

GALÁPAGOS ISLANDS
(Ecuador)

ECUADOR

Equator

SOUTH
AMERICA

PERU

BRAZIL

AMERICAN
SAMOA
(United
States)

COOK
ISLANDS
(New
Zealand)

SAMOA

FRENCH POLYNESIA
(France)

BOLIVIA

PARAGUAY

TONGA

Tropic of Capricorn

PITCAIRN ISLAND
(U.K.)

ARGENTINA

URUGUAY

CHILE

0   2000 mi

0   2000 km

FALKLAND
ISLANDS
(U.K.)

CENTRAL AMERICA AND WEST INDIES

Antarctic Circle

FLORIDA
(United States)

Gulf of Mexico

ATLANTIC
OCEAN

Tropic of Cancer

BAHAMAS

TURKS & CAICOS
ISLANDS
(United Kingdom)

CUBA

VIRGIN IS.
(United Kingdom)

MEXICO

CAYMAN IS.
(United Kingdom)

PUERTO RICO
(United States)

ST. KITTS & NEVIS

ANTIGUA &
BARBUDA

HAITI

DOMINICAN
REPUBLIC

BELIZE

GUADELOUPE
(France)

JAMAICA

VIRGIN IS. (United States)

GUATEMALA

MONTSERRAT (United Kingdom)

DOMINICA

MARTINIQUE
(France)

HONDURAS

Caribbean Sea

ST. LUCIA

EL
SALVADOR

0   400 mi

NETHERLANDS ANTILLES
(Netherlands)

ST. VINCENT &
THE GRENADINES

BARBADOS

NICARAGUA

0   400 km

ARUBA (Netherlands)

GRENADA

TRINIDAD
& TOBAGO

PACIFIC
OCEAN

COSTA
RICA

PANAMA

COLOMBIA

VENEZUELA

GUYANA

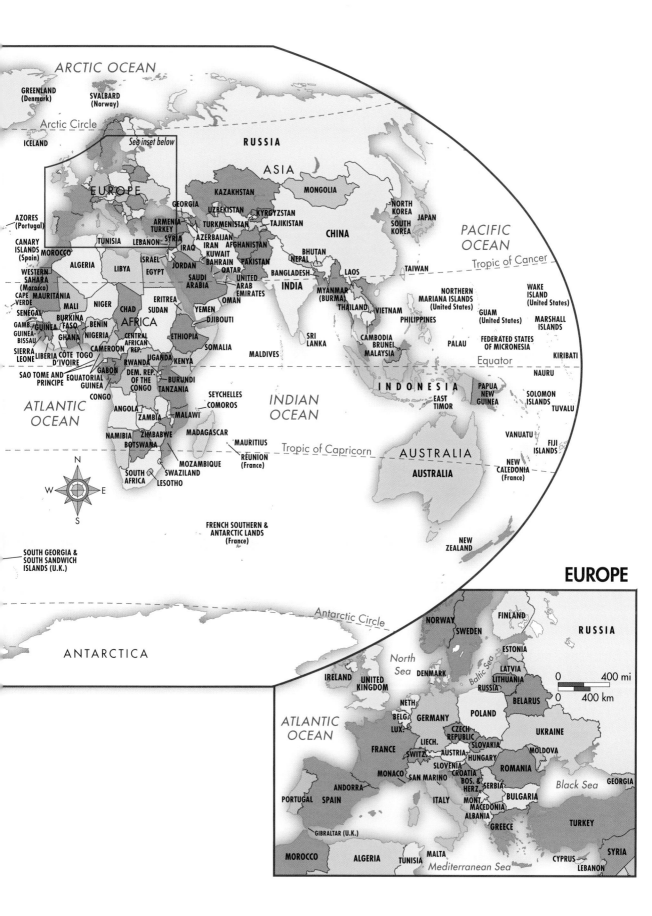

ARCTIC OCEAN

GREENLAND
(Denmark)

SVALBARD
(Norway)

Arctic Circle

ICELAND

RUSSIA

ASIA

EUROPE

See inset below

AZORES
(Portugal)

CANARY
ISLANDS
(Spain)

TUNISIA

MOROCCO

WESTERN
SAHARA
(Morocco)

ALGERIA

LIBYA

CAPE
VERDE

MAURITANIA

MALI

NIGER

SENEGAL

GAMB.
GUINEA-
BISSAU

GUINEA

BURKINA
FASO

CHAD

AFRICA

GEORGIA

ARMENIA
TURKEY
SYRIA

KAZAKHSTAN

UZBEKISTAN

TURKMENISTAN

AZERBAIJAN
IRAN
IRAQ

LEBANON

ISRAEL
JORDAN

EGYPT

ERITREA
SUDAN

YEMEN

DJIBOUTI

KYRGYZSTAN

TAJIKISTAN

MONGOLIA

NORTH
KOREA

SOUTH
KOREA

JAPAN

CHINA

AFGHANISTAN
KUWAIT
BAHRAIN
QATAR

PAKISTAN

SAUDI
ARABIA

UNITED
ARAB
EMIRATES

OMAN

BHUTAN

NEPAL

BANGLADESH

INDIA

MYANMAR
(BURMA)

LAOS

THAILAND

VIETNAM

TAIWAN

PACIFIC
OCEAN

Tropic of Cancer

WAKE
ISLAND
(United States)

NORTHERN
MARIANA ISLANDS
(United States)

GUAM
(United States)

PHILIPPINES

MARSHALL
ISLANDS

SIERRA
LEONE

LIBERIA

GHANA

CÔTE
D'IVOIRE

BENIN

NIGERIA

TOGO

CENTRAL
AFRICAN
REP.

CAMEROON

ETHIOPIA

SOMALIA

SRI
LANKA

MALDIVES

CAMBODIA
BRUNEI
MALAYSIA

PALAU

FEDERATED STATES
OF MICRONESIA

KIRIBATI

SAO TOME AND
PRINCIPE

EQUATORIAL
GUINEA

GABON

CONGO

RWANDA

UGANDA

DEM. REP.
OF THE
CONGO

KENYA

BURUNDI

TANZANIA

Equator

NAURU

INDONESIA

EAST
TIMOR

PAPUA
NEW
GUINEA

SOLOMON
ISLANDS

TUVALU

ATLANTIC
OCEAN

ANGOLA

ZAMBIA

MALAWI

SEYCHELLES

COMOROS

INDIAN
OCEAN

VANUATU

FIJI
ISLANDS

NAMIBIA

ZIMBABWE

BOTSWANA

MADAGASCAR

MAURITIUS

RÉUNION
(France)

Tropic of Capricorn

AUSTRALIA

AUSTRALIA

NEW
CALEDONIA
(France)

N
W   E
S

SOUTH
AFRICA

MOZAMBIQUE
SWAZILAND
LESOTHO

FRENCH SOUTHERN &
ANTARCTIC LANDS
(France)

NEW
ZEALAND

SOUTH GEORGIA &
SOUTH SANDWICH
ISLANDS (U.K.)

Antarctic Circle

ANTARCTICA

EUROPE

NORWAY

SWEDEN

FINLAND

RUSSIA

North
Sea

IRELAND

UNITED
KINGDOM

DENMARK

Baltic Sea

ESTONIA

LATVIA

LITHUANIA

RUSSIA

BELARUS

0   400 mi
0   400 km

ATLANTIC
OCEAN

NETH.

BELG.

LUX.

GERMANY

POLAND

CZECH
REPUBLIC

UKRAINE

FRANCE

LIECH.

SWITZ.

AUSTRIA

SLOVAKIA

HUNGARY

MOLDOVA

MONACO

SLOVENIA

CROATIA

ROMANIA

SAN MARINO

BOS. &
HERZ.

SERBIA

ANDORRA

MONT.

BULGARIA

Black Sea

GEORGIA

PORTUGAL

SPAIN

ITALY

MACEDONIA

ALBANIA

TURKEY

GIBRALTAR (U.K.)

GREECE

SYRIA

MOROCCO

ALGERIA

TUNISIA

MALTA

CYPRUS

LEBANON

Mediterranean Sea

Glossary

demography (deh-MAH-gra-fee) the study of the human population and the factors that affect it, such as births, deaths, and life expectancy

economic development (ee-kuh-NOM-ik di-VEL-uhp-muhnt) the change of the nature of an economy toward a greater reliance on industry and technology

family planning (FAM-lee PLAN-ing) methods used to limit the number and spacing of births by natural means or by the use of modern contraceptives

human rights (HYOO-muhn RITES) the idea that people have certain rights no matter where they live and which the government should not interfere with, such as the right to work, to health care, and to speak freely

immigration (im-uh-GRAY-shuhn) the movement of people from one country into another country

innovation (in-uh-VAY-shuhn) the creation of new things or new ways of doing things

migration (my-GRAY-shuhn) the movement of people from one area or country to another

natural resources (NAH-chuh-ruhl ri-SORSS) things found in nature that are used by humans for practical economic purposes, such as forests, water, coal, oil, and natural gas

pesticides (PESS-tuh-sydz) chemical substances used on crops to kill or prevent unwanted plants, bugs, or fungi

pollution (puh-LOO-shuhn) the releasing of harmful substances into the natural environment, which can damage that environment and cause health problems for humans

population density (pop-yuh-LAY-shuhn DEN-si-tee) the number of people living in a particular area

population policies (pop-yuh-LAY-shuhn POL-uh-seas) government programs aimed at stabilizing or reducing the population size; these may include family planning services and education, financial incentives to have smaller families, and limits on immigration

sustainable development (suh-STAYN-uh-buhl di-VEL-uhp-muhnt) methods of economic activity, such as construction or industry, which can be used over a long period of time without harming the natural environment

technology (tek-NOL-uh-jee) the use of science to benefit commercial or industrial goals

FOR MORE INFORMATION

Books

Bowden, Rob. *Cities*. San Diego: KidHaven Press, 2004.

Mason, Paul. *Population*. Chicago: Heinemann Library, 2006.

Obadina, Tunde. *Population and Overcrowding*.
Philadelphia: Mason Crest Publishers, 2007.

Web Sites

Wide Angle Growing Up Global—Kid Cards: Numbers Affecting Children Worldwide
www.pbs.org/wnet/wideangle/shows/global/cards.html
Information on how population growth affects the lives of kids around the world

Population Connection: Population Education
www.populationeducation.org
Information on overpopulation for students of all ages and resources for teachers

United Nations Population Fund—Population Issues: Meeting Development Goals
www.unfpa.org/pds/facts.htm
Facts about overpopulation and its effects around the world

U.S. Census Bureau
www.census.gov
All kinds of numbers and statistics, including United States and world population clocks

INDEX

Bangladesh, 10–11, 12, 15, 17, 19, 27

carrying capacity, 25
census, 5
China, 5, 6, 23, 24

demographers, 5, 7, 10, 14, 17
demographic age, 17
Denmark, 5

economic migrants, 20
economy, 11, 14, 19, 20, 23, 27
ecosystems, 25
education, 24, 25, 26, 27
energy resources, 7, 27

family planning, 24–25
farming, 11, 14, 15, 16, 19, 20, 27
food, 6, 7, 10, 11, 14, 15, 16, 25, 27

governments, 5, 14, 17, 21, 22, 23–24, 25, 26
Great Leap Forward, 23

Hong Kong, China, 5, 6, 14, 19
housing, 6, 10, 20

immigration, 20, 21
Indonesia, 19
innovation, 16, 17, 27
Iran, 24–25

Japan, 11, 17, 19
jobs, 11, 19, 20, 23

Malthus, Thomas, 14, 16
manufacturing, 19
Mexico, 20, 24
migration, 19, 20

natural resources, 7
numerical facts, 17

"one-child policy," 23, 24

pesticides, 11, 14
pollution, 6, 11, 16–17, 27
population density, 10, 14
population growth, 6, 8, 11–12, 14, 17, 19, 20, 21, 22, 23, 25–26, 27
population policies, 22, 23–24, 25

rivers, 11

seacoasts, 11

trade, 19
transportation, 11, 17

United States, 10, 19, 20

ABOUT THE AUTHOR

Robert Green has written more than 30 books for students. He is a regular contributor to publications on East Asia by the Economist Intelligence Unit and holds graduate degrees from New York University and Harvard University.